Calling the
BELOVED

INSPIRATIONAL POEMS

Calling the BELOVED

INSPIRATIONAL POEMS
Theresiu Janicki-Hardy

Copyright © 2013 Theresiu Janicki-Hardy.

All rights reserved. No part of this book may be used or reproduced by any means, graphic, electronic, or mechanical, including photocopying, recording, taping or by any information storage retrieval system without the written permission of the publisher except in the case of brief quotations embodied in critical articles and reviews.

Cover design and illustrations
by the author

Balboa Press books may be ordered through booksellers or by contacting:

Balboa Press
A Division of Hay House
1663 Liberty Drive
Bloomington, IN 47403
www.balboapress.com
1-(877) 407-4847

Because of the dynamic nature of the Internet, any web addresses or links contained in this book may have changed since publication and may no longer be valid. The views expressed in this work are solely those of the author and do not necessarily reflect the views of the publisher, and the publisher hereby disclaims any responsibility for them.

The author of this book does not dispense medical advice or prescribe the use of any technique as a form of treatment for physical, emotional, or medical problems without the advice of a physician, either directly or indirectly. The intent of the author is only to offer information of a general nature to help you in your quest for emotional and spiritual well-being. In the event you use any of the information in this book for yourself, which is your constitutional right, the author and the publisher assume no responsibility for your actions.

Any people depicted in stock imagery provided by Thinkstock are models, and such images are being used for illustrative purposes only.
Certain stock imagery © Thinkstock.

Printed in the United States of America.

ISBN: 978-1-4525-7761-6 (sc)
ISBN: 978-1-4525-7762-3 (hc)
ISBN: 978-1-4525-7763-0 (e)

Library of Congress Control Number: 2013912266

Balboa Press rev. date: 8/23/2013

CONTENTS

Welcoming You ix

Longing 1

Rebirth 43

Loving 75

Surrendering 123

Receiving 161

*Dedicated
to my beloved Guru
Paramahansa Yogananda
and to all seekers of the Beloved.*

WELCOMING YOU

I welcome you to share a journey with me through the valleys and up the mountains of our lives, from the depth of our human feelings to the joy of soaring with the Divine Companion who is always with us, guiding and blessing us.

These poems were written over many years, but mostly during the last year when I was tested deeply through being unwell and needing to let go for a time of all I had so carefully built through many years of counseling, teaching meditation and self-help courses and organizing retreats.

Although on a deep spiritual journey for many years and with the great good fortune of having a wonderful Guru, I dived into a deep well, where in my despair I found the light of the Divine Friend waiting for me, always supporting and gently guiding me. Slowly I was allowed to begin to blossom again, having many sweet embraces and connections on the way.

These poems are a reflection of these connections in which the joy of the communion and the grief of its seeming absence at other times are expressed. The poems poured from me, often several in a row, sometimes after deep meditation, at other times during sleepless nights or as tears flowed freely. I read some of these poems to my husband and my friends who were moved and felt they expressed feelings they also experienced. Through these encouragements and a feeling of wishing to share with others, I offer these words in the hope they may bring you joy and encouragement.

Our journeys are all highly individual, but often share many common experiences. We all come from the same source of Light and we are all sparks of that Light returning to the Father/Mother from whom we came into being. At times we are lost in the trials of life and our personalities, in the little and larger dramas of our relationships and lives. Yet we are always loved and are never less than Divine.

May you find upliftment and joy in reading these poems while travelling your journey - *our* journey - back to the One we truly are!

With love, light and blessings,

Theresiu.

LONGING

LIKE A CHILD

O, Lord let me be
like a child again
playing free in Your garden
plucking flowers of devotion
to lay at Your divine feet.

O, may I be like a child again
playing in Thy fields
of the eternal Now
picking daisies to make a necklace
to garland Thee
finding in each flower
Your smile for me.

O, Lord may I always feel
Your touch of love in my heart
set me free to dance for You
the dance of joy and love
to know Your child I will always be.

FOR YOU

One day
I will dance again
in joy

I will dance with You alone
Seeing You alone
everywhere
in all and all things

Your sweet hand
touching my tear stained face
and Your lips resting on
my head
where a lotus bloom
will blossom in its full glory
which I will pluck
to lay at Your
beloved divine feet

MY LONGING FOR THEE

In pain I found
my longing for Thee
enlarged and washed in tears
my heart was aching
for Your sweet solace
a touch of Your presence.

Today a gift of joy
Your presence sweet as a smile
so peaceful, so grateful,
such sober, such still and
deep sweet joy.

I love You my beloved Lord
I bow at Your feet
come to me as pain
come to me as joy
whatever way You choose
but promise that
You come to me, always.

LIKE THE FLUTE OF KRISHNA

O Lord let me be like
Your flute,
empty and clean,
through which You can play
a song of Love and Beauty
into this world.

O, Lord, make me
an instrument
of Your Love, Peace and Joy.

OCEAN OF PEACE

With outstretched arms,
with Your voice of stillness
You are always calling me
You are always waiting for me
to return to You,
where my soul belongs
and finds its peace.
A peace so deep
A peace that passes
all understanding.

My restless being
finds rest at last
in You.
When, o when
will I learn to surrender?
Why play in the land of mind
while Your ocean of
eternal loving peace
is my home?

HELP ME TO SHINE

Mud covers the diamond.
I want to shine.
I no longer want to be like a moon,
with its seasonal changes of darkness and light.
I want to be a sun.
A star in Your firmament
steady and light and bright
reflecting and shining Your light
as You intended me to Be.

O, my Beloved, I do not know
how to talk to You.
Forgive me, love me, be with me,
help me, I love You.
Aum, Aum, Aum.

TEACH ME

Teach me to drink
from the fountain of
Your thirst quenching love
which flows within my Soul.

Teach me to meditate on You
and merge my Soul with You
into the Oneness of Being.

EMBRACE ME

I want to kiss
with the abundance of my love
the dust of Your feet
surrendering in self-forgetfulness
like John kissed the feet of Christ.

Will You pull me up
and embrace me, Lord?
I so long for Your kiss on my forehead
to see Your golden star of light
reflected in Your loving smile.

Burst my heart
with love for You alone
Melt away all boundaries
Let me be in You
like a star in Your sky
I cannot bear this separation any longer.

DANCE WITH ME

You are the Creator
the creator of all
Dance with me
dance through me
surfing the waves of the ocean of life
Dance with me
in the silence of my soul
Sing in the joy of my heart
Bless me
Bless through me
all who walk my path
in and through Your grace

AT HIS FEET

I found in Rumi's treasure trove
the same longing and pain
as in my own

It seems that suffering
the pain of this longing
this lonely separation
the long and sleepless nights
the seeming absence of His presence
is all part of this journey

Do not give up
for your next step
may take you to His Feet
where kissing them
you shall see His face
reflected in the tears
dropping from your eyes

And you realize
He was there, always
waiting for you
to surrender

SPEAK TO ME

Speak to me
Touch my heart
with Your Love.
Let me dwell
in Your Being.
Let me rest
my head on Your
sacred breast.

HOW MANY TIMES?

Seeking distractions,
why not look
for You?

You who are
the Source of my being,
You seem so far away.
Why did I dwell
on the littleness of life,
the lesser manifestations
of Your life force,
why did I not look
for You?

How many times
will I feel empty handed
because life was flowing away
like water through a sieve?

Why do I not
hold You closer
and dwell in my heart
of hearts where You live?

Help me, call me,
carry me Home
to You!
Only You!
No longer trapped
by the snares
of existence
the ups and downs of life
I wish to dwell
in You
who art my Love
and my Beloved.

BE WITH ME

I scream in agony
on my self-made cross
do not forsake me
Be with me
in this hour of need.

Tear me apart
I scream and struggle
but in the end
what a relief
to just Be in You.

Guide me, bless me
Be with me.
I hate You, I hate myself
I love You, I love myself
Yin and Yang forsaken
in the eternal circle
of Your precious Now.

CLIMBING THE LADDER

Slowly I climb
the steps of this ladder
slipping and sliding
backwards,
clutching on
crying and howling,
steadying and re-finding
my way up to You.
Up and down
and up and down.
Yet I will
never give up
until I reach Thee.

Stretch out Your hand
help me up
like a child by its father.
Keep me safe
in Your love for me
and in my love
for You.

LET ME BE

Let me be like the lark
spiraling ever closer
to Thee
singing Thy song of Joy
in total surrender
with all my being.

RESCUE ME!

Whirlpools of feelings
pull me down.
How do you get
out of a whirlpool?
You need to go down
all the way
and then swim away.

Will I be able to swim away
or will I drown?
Save me then
or let me drown
in this drama of life.

That is all it is -
a drama on the stage of life.
See yourself as an actor
in the centre of your stage.
But God and Guru
are the directors.

What is the script?
I do not know the lines!
That is it:
I do not know the lines.
If I did it would not be entertaining,
it would not provide me with growth.

God and Guru know the lines,
they know the script
and they took me on!
So, let me play the script
they give me, well
each day again.
So, right now
I am a drowning man,
or a woman rather,
gasping for my breath.

Put out your hand
and be rescued!
That is all it takes.
Put out your hand
and be rescued and saved.
How do I put out my hand?
Give God and Guru a Soul call.
They will hear.
Trust that they hear.

O, Master
You seem so far away.
Open my heart.
I know that I love You!
Help me,
Help me as You wish
to the deepest unraveling
through this darkness of ignorance.
Nothing else.

SHOW ME YOUR FACE

Electric karmic currents
rush through my body
Burning needles stitch my brain
A fire is raging in my head
I cry out to You.
O, Lord, when I call
hear my prayer.
You must come!

Show me Your face of love
Show me Your face of compassion
Reveal Yourself
Reveal Yourself to me.
Don't leave me here, alone.

My Master says You are
the nearest of the near
the dearest of the dear
Be Thou my nearest
Be Thou my dearest
Let me melt in Your love.

Burn my body to ashes
if You must
but save my soul
in Your love.

THOU AND I

I need to create space again
Space to Be
Leaving the world behind
to enter in communion with Thee

Only Thou and I
dancing on the waves
of the great ocean of life

SLEEPLESS NIGHTS

Reading Rumi last night
I was reading myself:
Reflections of love
and longing and pain.
It seems to be part of the journey.
He too speaks of sleepless nights,
His Guru smiles and says
You don't pray enough!

Do I pray enough?
No. I must pray more
and feel love
and be loved.
So simple, why make it more complicated?
How I am hanging on
to this veil I call myself.
Let it go, let it be torn apart
for in the emptiness
you will find Yourself.

TO GOD!

I love You
Always.
Even when I go
through the valleys of shame
and leaves of
past karma fall upon me.
I love You always
when I stumble
and forget Thee
and when I
embrace Thee
in shining glory.

Allow me to come home
beloved Father
soon!
I cannot wait
any more
I have longed for You
for so long.
I am tired and weary
from the journey.

Embrace me,
Love me,
Allow me to know
that You love me!
I love You always.

REBIRTH

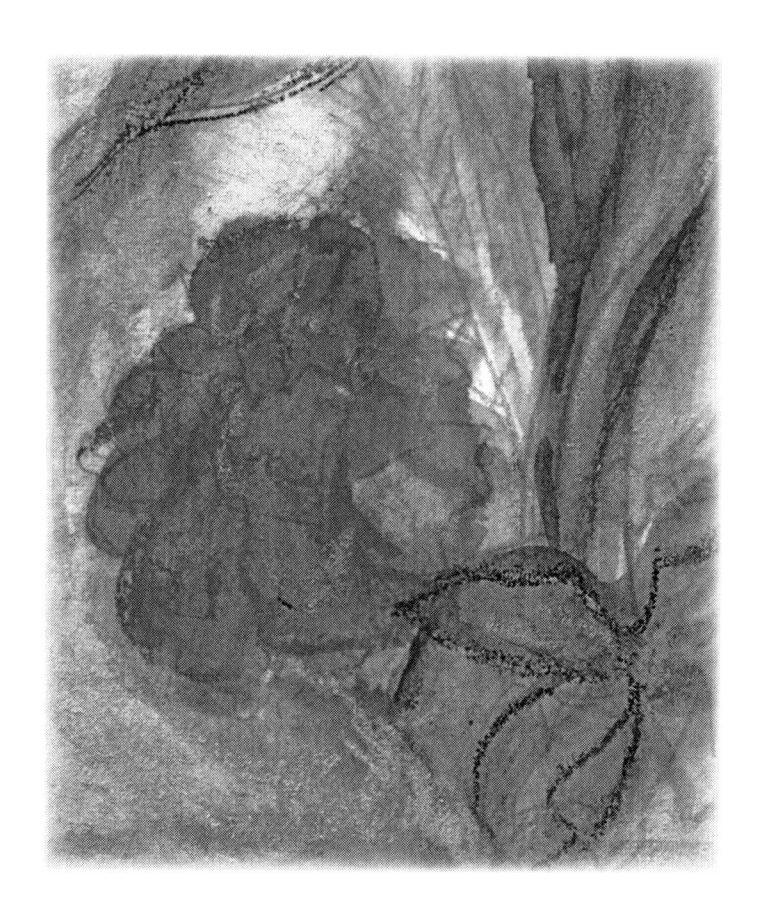

ON WINGS OF LIGHT

Let the process happen
No effort
Make the journey into Being
slowing into a new rhythm
and pattern of being
A new paradigm
without fear.

No guilt required here
Let go of the guilt
the guilt that you were born,
the guilt that you are alive.
Let it all dissolve
No more fear and guilt
in the fuel tank of living
Just joy and love.

I shall by flying
How amazing
I have been a caterpillar
with glimpses of the ecstasy
of my being and potential
Now I will be a butterfly
I will fly and be free
What joy, what prospect.

A divine butterfly
with wings of light
Your light
Your flight!

THE MIRACLE OF BIRTH

Dying is still taking place
Yet being born and dying
are intimately related.

When you die
to the caterpillar,
metamorphosis for the butterfly begins.
When you die
to the astral
you descend into the womb.

It is in dying
that the formation
of the new really begins.
Then birth is death
to the phase of life
in the cocoon,
to the fetus stage
and the transformation
is the new born
divine miracle
of life.

So have I been born again?
Not quite yet.
You are still in the womb.
The membrane is breaking
and the birth canal is opening.

Die, die then to the old self
and allow the hurricane of God's will
to take you through the birth canal
into the final push.

To be born into His light
and be renewed
according to His will and design.
Surrender, surrender, surrender
have faith, have faith,
have faith.

UNITED

I love You
I love myself
I finally love myself!

I was born to love myself.
When I finally could see
and take responsibility for this,
when I finally,
totally bathed
in the tears of forgiveness
of myself and others,
I was born
to myself
In You.

Bliss and Love united
in Your divine arms.
May all experience this love and joy
so sweet
so complete
so tender.

I am born
a Child Divine
in and of You
United and One
Always.

NEW BEGINNINGS

Today You taught me
that in each halt
is a new beginning
Surrender to not walking
surrender to whatever You bring
for You smile at me
in my heart
in the flowers and trees.

You speak to me in
the sounds of silence
and in the roaring power
of Your oceanic voice within
and when You gently
sing a song for me
in the robin in my tree.

You, who are within me
reflecting Your beauty
in so many ways
wherever I look
reflecting Your love
in so many faces
and gifts of gentleness
You are the Beloved
of my heart.

Whispering in the song of silence
smiling with Your
smile of light
carrying me on the wings
of Your angels
I am content
and joyfully surrender
waiting each moment
for Your tender touch
of infinite love.

NAKED

Stripped naked
to my bare wood

Now strengthen
your roots
in God and Guru

Then the blossoming can
occur with renewed
vigour and beauty
in honour to Him alone

LIKE A RIVER

Let it flow
Let it grow
It will become a river
which will carry you
to the sea
Divine Mother's sea.

I am so tired,
so deeply tired of fighting
I no longer want to fight
this illness of resistance
in manifestation.

What am I resisting?
Who am I resisting?
What is so glorious about the me
I am holding onto
Why not die
so I can be reborn
in You?

O, teach me how to die
how to surrender
and be born again
in You.

A THOUGHT DIVINE

I was born
a thought
of Your Divine Mind
A spark of light
emerging from Your Heart
A little circle
in Your whirling spirals
of creation
A Child Divine
being into Being
ever connected
ever protected
Held in Your arms
of Light

BIRTHING

To this cause I was born
through all the suffering
through all the pain,
the violence, turbulence,
love, hate, blood,
tears, some laughter,
much, much suffering,
overwhelm, lovers, rejection,
pushing, pulling, births, deaths,
storms, lives within lives.

All a great birthing
into the eternal now.
Forgiving, understanding
myself, my earthly parents
and all with whom I repeated
and danced this earth life.

All melted into the bliss
of the birth
of the Divine Child
that I truly am.

BURNING THE DROSS

What is going on?
The dross is burning
Accept.
One day it will be done.
Keep praying, keep hoping.
It will pass.

What would Jesus tell me?
I am with you in this trial
Trust in me
Hold fast to your Guru
He will see you through
Divine Mother's hand, though casting a shadow
is stretched out in blessing.

The blessings will become apparent
as you walk the path
of this underground cave
which is so dark.

In the centre of the cave
when you will least expect it
you will find the light of Divine Mother
waiting to embrace you.
Be sure of this.
Don't doubt
All will be well.

Walk slowly and carefully
don't try to hasten your process
for each step has a gift.
You are not alone
yet only you can walk this path alone.
Angels are with you
Listen to your Inner guidance
and the voice within
will lead you
through God's and Guru's grace back
to the land of the truly living.

This trial is a great gift,
much will be gained
and much will be lost.
Don't grieve for what you have to leave behind
and rejoice in what will be given to you.

Be patient, have courage, have faith.
You are loved deeply and profoundly.
You are in Me
I am in You
All is well.

FOR BABAJI

I dreamed of Babaji
Angel of Light
flying through the sky

He gave me a glimpse
of His Being
honoured I am
even in a dream

O, Babaji, Prince of Light
I bow at Your feet
Come to me
and touch my heart

May the burning bush
of this pain and suffering
be healed by Your touch
of divine love

May I heal
from ignorance and be forgiven
for straying so many incarnations
from my Beloved One
dreaming in the dungeons
while covering in mud
the glory of the gift
of my true Being

Touch me then, O, Babaji
through Your hand and
the sweet grace of my Guru
that I may arise
baptized anew
in Your light

Aum Babaji
I love You
I bow to You
great manifestation of the Divine
What grace that I may
know Your name
and see Your face
through the gift of my Guru

I bow at Your divine
ever youthful feet
I lay my head in the dust
made by Your tread
ashes to ashes go
and the phoenix may arise
and fly free
on wings of light
through Your blessing

FREE YOURSELF

Free yourself from the rut.
lift yourself above the clouds
of your mind
into the light of my/Your Being.
I love You!

FORGIVENESS

This morning meditation
You came so gently and sweetly
blessing me with Your light and love.

But first I had to face my past,
reams of past searching for love,
mistakes, abuses, so many things
so painful to watch,
this parade of past errors
marching through my consciousness.

Facing it
I asked You for forgiveness,
forgiving myself
I moved into my love for You,
away from this ocean of suffering
as Krishna calls this.
No longer attuning myself to it
I see, bless and release all,
blessing and releasing myself.
This was a different time
a different life.

Now let the love of God
and Master
heal the scars.
Mary Magdalene was not only

redeemed by Jesus,
she became one of His most exalted disciples
who had the grace
to be the first to see Him
after His arising.

Master and God have forgiven me
I am here, with Them,
In the light
and on the spiritual pathway.
How blessed I am.

Baptized in purifying tears
I set myself free.
Thank You for rescuing me
beloved God and Master.
Thank You for making me see
that I am the Soul,
ever One with Thee
untainted, unscarred
by life or death,
ever shining in my Oneness
with Thee.

I NO LONGER WISH TO HIDE

I wish no longer to hide
from You
To hide my inferiority
behind the grandness
of position and wisdom.

I no longer wish
to be great
I am facing myself
Undoing and unpicking
my walls of defense
my strategic plans
of survival of this I.

I wish to be innocent
like a child
Your divine child
to be free
and rise again
in You.

JUST YOU AND ME

My identity
is being stripped away
layers have been peeled
It was bloody
and painful
Tears and blood commingled
in streams
carrying my old self away.
I finally died today
I died to my old, outer self.
I stood naked
before You.

I am Your disciple
I am Your child
Your chela
Yours
Nothing else matters
I finally let go
It is happening
Emptiness, just You and Me.
Blessed Spirit I am He.

GREAT MOTHER

O, Great Mother, as Your sea gives rise
to its dancing waves,
each wave continuing to be part of Your eternal sea,
so all form conscious or subconscious
is always part of
Thine eternal unmanifested Source.

Thy great Cosmic light manifesting so many vibrations
in Thine amazing creation,
with our brain an important gift to us
for Thy expression
into this world of matter,
each particle a cosmic scientific wondrous miracle
in its form and function alike.

Conscious and subconscious thought,
vision, touch, taste, hearing, walking,
dreaming, dancing –
all an inspiration from Your great beyond.

Each seemingly inauspicious manifestation
a cosmic performance of great wonder and
the gentle touch of Your great Love,
which holds all of creation together
until You call us back
to Your light-filled Womb.

LOVING

GIFT OF LOVE

O, Gift of love
in gentle waves
of golden light
You embrace me
telling me of Your
love for me.
Tender beauty
of warming sweetness
gold and lilac symphonies
accompanied by
the eternal soothing drum
of Your loving voice.

Engulfing ecstasy
bursting my heart
beyond its confining boundaries
of self into You,
eternal You.

IN GRATITUDE

In eternal gratitude
I bow at Your holy feet
I kiss them with
tears of love.
How can I even begin
to thank You?

You who are my Mother,
my Guru, my most beloved Friend.
You who baptize me
with the love of Your heart
which melts all boundaries
of ego away,
who love me enough
to roast me in the fires
of Your terrible love
to clean me and empty me
so I can be filled
with You
Only You.

You who never give up on me
Always forgiving
Always encouraging
Always waiting
patiently

for me to return
when I wander away
in the garden of delusion.

You who sit by my side
when I cry the tears of pain
of the tests and trials
for Your love.
May I always see
and feel Your love.

I tell You
that I love You
Feeling and melting and
knowing the river of this love
that flows through my heart
to be one with the ocean
of Your Love.

For You and I
are One
Inseparably, always One.
What bliss
What joy
to know I am Yours
inseparably One
In Love.

LIVING FOR LOVE

Just live for love alone
Write poems of love
to the Beloved of your heart
Dance in His glory
Paint reflections of your love
for His face
Love Him in all you meet
and in yourself.

Bow at His feet
at the feet of your Guru
Smile at Him in the flowers
Feel His warmth in the sun
Love Him in all
life's joys and sufferings.

YOU ALONE

I want to cross the bridge
from me to You
I want to dwell
where You live and have Your home
I don't want to think of me
but of You alone

For You are the star
of my Being
You create the firmament
and all that is
You are the song
and the singer
You are the melody
and the sound

You play us into being
through your flute of love
accompanied by the drum
of the ocean
You are the beauty
in all beings and all things
You are the life

that flows through creation's veins
You are the greatest
and the humblest of all
Your smile is the light
within all things

You are the Lover
behind all Love
and the Love within all lovers
You are the colours
in the rainbow
and the song of the nightingale

You, O Beloved
You, my heavenly Father
You, my sweetest divine Mother
You, my eternal Friend
You, who are the You in all
and everything
and the beat in my heart
the prayer on my lips
whispering to Yourself
that I love You

THY WORD OF LOVE

O my God, I love You so
I dance on my toes
reaching for heaven
for You,
plucking a star of love
to lay at Your divine feet.
Caresses of Your love
touch my heart
in the song of the birds,
the beauty of the flowers
nodding their heads
in the gentle breeze
of Your sweet smelling breath.

O my God, I love You so
I love You so
my heart is bursting
its boundaries
of confinement
and melts in Thee
becoming the stars, birds
and flowers of everywhere
where You are.

O my God, I love You so
I intertwine the flute
of my voice
through which You sing
my song of love for You
with the sound of Thine
Oceanic Being
melting into One Word.

Thy Word of Love everywhere
manifesting into Thy glorious Being.
O my God, I love You so.

SONG OF LOVE

I love writing
but above all
I love writing about Thee.
I love inspiring
but above all
I love inspiring about Thee.

I love when Your voice
echoes through my voice,
Your love beats in my heart,
when like a lark
I fly on wings of light
carried by Thy wind
singing to You, to Thee
with You, with Thee
the song of Thy glory.

The song of Thy love
given within and without
through Thy peace,
Thy light, Thy Holy Voice
Thy smile in all smiles
and all gestures of love
become an ocean of
Thine unceasing love for me.
Offered in return at
Thy Holy Feet
as I whisper my song
of unending love to Thee.

THIS VALENTINE'S DAY

I love You Lord
On this Valentine's Day
I lay my heart before You
May all tears
change into roses
of eternal love

Each tear shed
change into a smile
of gratitude and love
for You

Each battle scar
an emblem which I offer
in joy of new found peace
in You

I love You always
in You
in all
and in me!

PLAY YOUR TUNE

Whisper and tug on
the strings of my heart.
Play the tune of Your
Chant of Love.
Ring the bells
of Your church
in my heart
for You alone
Everywhere.

MAY I BE WORTHY

How fortunate I am
to know Love
to feel the touch
of You in my heart
Your loving fingers
kneading the dough
of my life
into bread.

May the bread
of the Christ life
be tasted by my Soul.
May I be baptized
in Your Light
where I may quell
the thirst of my heart
with Your blood
You offered us
when alive as Jesus
and through the Masters.

May I be worthy
to kiss Your feet
and anoint them
with my love.
Never leave my side
for without You
I am not.

INDICATIONS OF LOVE

You spoke to me today
so sweetly
so encouragingly
through several different voices
You gave me
such indication of Your love.
It moved me
to tears.
Tears of sweet gratitude.
I bow to You
with all my love.

FREEDOM FROM FEAR

I now release fear
I let go of worry.
I now live only from love.
Love is the guiding force of
my Inner Voice.
Love is of God
Love is God
God is Love.
I am one with God
I am Love.
Love dissolves all fear
I dissolve all fear into the love of God.

From this day,
this moment onwards
I commit myself to Love,
I commend myself to Love.

I step out of the land of fear,
through the golden gateway
into the land of Love.

Below lies my life
as I have lived it, fear.
It pushed me up the mountain
here I stand,
I bless my life
all the people I have loved
I step through the gateway now
into the land of Love.

EMBRACING THE BELOVED

O, my Divine Beloved
Source of my Being
I bow to You
with all my love
in gratitude for my life
in the infinity of Your Being
where I may dance
as a shining star
in Your firmament of creation.

May my vibrational offering
to You and all in You
be one of light and joy
and peace and love and wellbeing
I love You
I embrace you, my Beloved
in this dance of life.

BLESSING OF LOVE

I love myself
I really love myself

I bless myself
I bless my body
I love my body
I love my life

My whole being is pervaded
by His presence
I love Him inside me

Thou and I never apart
I honour and love Thee
inside myself

My life is Your Life
Your Life is my life
How could I not be healed
for You are in me

I cannot be separate from You
I love You
I love me in You
and You in Me

Love, love, just Love

ASK AND IT SHALL BE GIVEN

Ask and it shall be given.
What shall I ask?
I ask for God Himself.

Then you must give your self.
Give all of your self to Him
and He shall give
Himself to you.

But give without expectation.
Give with all your heart
with all your might
and all your dedication
to Him
in your heart and mind
and in all you see.

Live again with passion,
a passion for Love,
for Love and God alone.
And ask humbly in your heart

for Him
to reveal Himself to you.
Ceaselessly, continuously
think of Him
and tell Him you love Him,
attuning yourself
to where He dwells
within you.

A SMILE JUST FOR YOU

Carried in an Ocean of Love
and gratitude
I bow my head
at Thy Feet.

You are my Saviour,
You are my Father,
my Mother,
my most beloved Friend.

You smile at me
through the eyes
of my Master
and all You send me
to love me and them.

You, who are present
in the beauty
of the flowers,
in the song
of the birds.

You who roar
in the ocean
and shine so warmly
in the friendly sun.

You who paint
the skies
in evanescent colours
and touch my face
in the breeze.

You created
a world for me
to walk in.
Let me walk then
with a smile on my face.
A smile just for You
in all
everywhere.

ANOINTMENT

O, my Lord,
I anoint Thy
beloved head
with the rose oils
of my love
for Thee.

I give Thee a rose,
made fragrant by Thee,
which I humbly picked
to lay at Thy feet.
You created it,
You created me,
so this moment
in time could occur.

In Your heart
You always knew
the time without time,
when I would melt again
in Thee.

Love becoming Love
Love loving Love
Love being Love
You calling me
Me calling You
You and me
Me and You
Beloved in eternal Love.

ONLY YOU!

I have a choice
What choice shall I make today?
I choose You
Only You!

ANSWERED PRAYER

I prayed to You
to let me feel Your Love
I prayed to You
to accept my love
and deepen my love for You,
for You alone.

I asked You to forgive me
for all my trespasses
against Your laws
but above all for
forgetting You,
for not living in You,
for not being with You
and wandering in the land
where ego rules
where matter soiled my mind.

O, my beloved Lord,
my beloved Divine Mother,
my beloved Christ and Krishna,
my Guru and all the Masters,
bless me with Your love
bless me with Your guidance
Let me know always
that I am one with You.

So sweetly You responded
with such gentle tender grace
I feel so blessed
I feel so loved
How I love You,
my tender, sweet beloved One.
You are rocking me
in Your arms of Love
in a tender embrace
of sweet pulsations
of Your light.

You came to me
and responded with such Love
to my prayer.
How blessed I am.
I love You
I love You
I love You
Beloved One in All
My beloved One
My dearest, beloved God.

MY FATHER, MY FATHER

You gave me through
the touch of his hand
and the sweetness of his smile
a glimpse of the love
You have for me.

Through his devotion
and hard work
You showed me
how You are always busy for me.

He showed me through his love
in a human way,
the way of the Father.
You gave him to me,
such a precious gift
of tenderness and kindness.

Now You have called him
back to one of Your
heavenly mansions.

You showed me
how he was enveloped
in love and light,
radiant with glory and joy.

I cried with happiness for him
whom I loved so dearly.
The sight of his brilliance
and smile of fulfillment
with joy eased my grief.

I know he is with You
my sweet Guru
I asked You to guide him there.

The pain is deep
I am surprised at my
moments of desolation.
Yet I know that You are
evermore with him and me
and his love and my love
are always present in You.

The love we shared
was You making
Yourself felt present
and tangible.

Now I must find You
ever deeper and evermore
in the vibrations of
light and sound,

where You eternally
call and caress me.

How You vibrated
Yourself into being
in such a wonderful way.
How I loved You
as my dear father,
O, beloved Father of mine.

*after the death of my beloved father Wiktor Janicki
on 7th April 2002*

ROCK ME THEN

Sleepless is my night,
I read through all
the wise things gathered
in these last months.
Through things You brought
to me from minds
wise and clear as channels
of Your love and wisdom.

So deeply I saw
and I was touched.
Yet so often again
I fall back
into the claws of despair
and believing in the smallness
of this body-self
with all its troubles.

How often do I need to fall
to learn to walk again
in the perfection
that I am?
Disbelieving any of the arrogance
of ego-made promises,
never leading to perfection and joy.

Holding Your hand alone,
safe in Your vision
of beauty and truth.
Seeing myself and others
just as You made us.
Shining Your radiance
Your light
Your perfection?

Help me then
Your helpless Child.
Lift me on Your lap
and cuddle me
rock me gently
rock all the fear
out of my heart
rock me then
into peace and silence
into Your safety
where within and without melt
into a sweet oneness
with You
where I surrender and dissolve
not just temporarily
but always in You.

Loving You,
Being with You
is the only way
which brings me happiness.
I love You, I always do.
Rock me then
so I feel Your love for me,
Your Child
Until there is only Love.

SILENT WAVES OF LOVE

The words that I use
to express my love
for Thee
are as useless coins
to buy the beauty
of paradise.

I can only
sit in Your love
in the stillness
where my love
touches the feet
of Your Love
and thrillingly sings
to You in silent waves
melting in Your ocean
of Love that is all Love.

THY TEMPLE

I am Thy temple warden
looking after this house of Thine
Instead of feeling sorry for myself
for every ill befalling me
I will cheerfully attend
to mending and
helping You to maintain
this little temple of mine
which is Thine, which is Thine.

Each ache I shall polish
with attention and mend where necessary
with love for Thee
knowing that all tools I need
will come to me
in divine right order.

The inner temple
of my thought gardens
I shall water
with love and cheerfulness
and joy in loving Thee
Weeding the weeds of negativity
and fear and worry
Plucking flowers of devotion
to lay at Your feet.

In the innermost sanctuary
of my Soul's altar
I will light candles of light
and dust away all indifference
I will place the golden lotus flower
of divine love
at the feet of Your presence
which I will kiss
with my tearstained face
in love and gratitude to Thee.

SURRENDERING

BE STILL

Be still and know that I am God
This is my task
to be still
Be still and know that I am God
for in that stillness He reveals Himself,
the secret that I AM

I am One with Him
inseparably One with Him
always have been, always will be
all else is an illusion,
a cover-up this dance of maya

Dance of Life and dance of death
dance of love and hate
dance of success and failure
all a dance, a masquerade

All is God
all is You
I am You, in stillness revealed
O, Love of my Love
reveal Yourself to me as I AM

I love You
I love myself
as You, as Me
as I AM

ON WINGS OF GRACE

The butterfly
struggles out of its cocoon
to give it strength to fly.
But flying it does!

I am emerging.
It has been a painful birth,
but I will fly
on wings of Your grace
into the light
of Your sun.

It is different
from how I thought
it would be.
Less glamorous,
more bitter sweet.

I need to surrender
to Your plan
for my life.
Letting go of my ideas
into the blueprint
You set out for my flight
into the light.

When I let go
and lay may head in Your lap,
so sweetly You carry me
up into Your light,
where all burdens melt away,
where all suffering
fades like a dream
and only the reality
of Being in You
exists.

Tears of Love,
Tears of joy,
My heart and soul belong to You,
to You alone!

I BELONG TO HIM

Nothing belongs to you
nothing is your own.
Don't cling to anything,
don't cling to your life
as you have known it.
It belonged to God anyway.
Now He has taken it back
It is fine.

I am now in waiting
in formation time.
His divine hands
will sculpt me
for my new life
which only belongs to Him.

The now belongs to Him
the eternal Now,
where I find Him
in my own heart
smiling His tender smile
of sweetest love.
Such grace, such beauty
I surrender,
for I belong to Him.

GREAT DANCER

Great Dancer
invite me
into Your spiral
of ever-deepening dance.

Move me into surrender.
Move me into eternal oneness
with You.
Vibrating, pulsating,
moving, flowing,
reaching, bending,
lying myself down
at Your feet.

Move me through
my struggling tears,
through the smile of my light,
leaping, skipping,
standing still,
melting into you.

Dance me
Great Dancer!
For You and I are
the dance-
the eternal dance
of life.

GIFTS OF YOU

I lay my head
at Your feet
in eternal gratitude.

You, who as my Father
take such tender care of me
and enfold me in Your loving arms.

You, who as my Mother
nourish me daily
with love and food
and the breath of life
and live within me.

You, who as my Friend
and Guardian Angel
walk beside me
guiding and encouraging me,
forgiving me lovingly,
understanding me
when no one else does.

You, who manifest to me
as beauty in the flowers
and the roses of my life.

You, who are born
in the cradle of my heart
as the baby Christ
and fill me with Your light
and Your love.
Ever expanding, all encompassing,
sweet divine love.

GENTLY IN MY SOUL

Not as passionate as before
I am milder
I have suffered
I have bled
The I has been eroded
somewhat.
Now gently in my Soul
I need to find Your guidance
Your voice alone
to move forward
on my Path through life.
Your life now!

Guide me then
and bless me
that I will walk on
until the end.
Never wavering
never giving up
and finding You
reflected everywhere,
but most of all
within my own heart

where I smile
with soft eyes
at Your sweet face
within.

Feeling my face
become Your face,
feeling Your face
become mine.
My whole being
melts in You,
inseparably One.

A PRAYER

O, Lord
I do not know how to pray
Teach my heart to pray
to live for You alone

Teach me to live a life of joy and love
expressing only Your beauty

Teach me to be free
and live like a child
carefree in Your Love and protection
Dancing in the Eternal Now

Teach me to surrender
and be in harmony with You

O, Lord, let Your song of love
flow through me
Make me an empty vessel
filled with the tune of Your voice of silence
where I found You
May my face only reflect You

DO DWELL IN ME

Why this pain?
Why this suffering?
Is this how I feel alive?
Is this Your will for me
or is this my distorted view
creating painful experiences?
Is this part of my Path?
Is this part of the necessary cleansing
before the new can arrive?
Is this part of the grinding
of the ego
the emptying and washing
of this old house,
so You may dwell in it?

O, do dwell in me,
fill this old house
with Your renewing light
and shine it blue and white
into the darkness of my life.

O, do dwell in me
and touch my heart often
with Your magic wand of Love,
washing away all delusions.

I wish to be free
in You.
Melt my wish with Yours
and guide me with Your vision.

Overshadow my little murmurings
and plans for my life.
No statues, no websites or books,
but a little place in Your heart.

No outer grandeur,
but inner finding
of You alone
my heart's desire.

DIE TO THIS SELF

I want to die to this I
die to this self
How do you die to this I?
The answer came swiftly:
think of God alone!
God, God, God,
your only thought.
Then the self will die,
like a little dog
which receives no treats,
it will go away.

I will live for You alone.
Touch me, shine through me,
be my strength, my love,
my vision, my wisdom,
my Being.

When I look in the mirror
I will only see Your face
smiling at me.
Wherever I look
only Your face
Your smile and love
in everyone and everything.

I love You, I love myself
I love myself, I love You.

ATTUNING TO THE HIGHEST

Whatever you attune to,
you become.
Be angry or negative,
identify with illness
and you attune
to that level of vibration.

So pray, meditate,
read the words
of the Holy Ones
Listen to the Aum vibration
everywhere
and you will become that.

Always attune to the highest
practising the presence of God
and the Great Ones
letting your consciousness
merge in theirs.

Becoming One
with what you are,
no longer diving in muddy waters
but expanding in
the cosmic sea of bliss.

CRYSTALS OF SOUL LIGHTS

Thou didst become Man
Thou didst become The Son
Giving Thyself to us, to me,
Visible exquisite light materialized
in my Christ, my Master
and in my Gurudeva.

Beautiful Swan of Love,
your exquisite wings
will carry me over oceans
of lifetimes of confusion
into the Light of Thy Being;
my Being.
Lift me up
allow me to Be Thou.

Crystals of soul lights
of Master and Guru You showed me.
My soul, free
from matter-bound ignorance
also glows in Thy love.
Allow me to dissolve
in that sparkling beauty
of Thy Being.
Allow me to be One with Thee,
Now and Always.

DWELL WHERE HE ABIDES

Dwell where He abides
Let go of all fear
Let your heart be made pure
and flooded by His love
Your love, all One
climbing the ladder of vibration
from fear into love
Love for the One
in whom you exist
All else is an illusion

MY GURU, MY DIVINE FRIEND

My Guru
I love you!
I want to go so much
deeper in my surrender
to you.
My most beloved
always forgiving
Divine Friend.
Forgive me then
the millions of times
I didn't trust you,
didn't have faith in you,
looked elsewhere for answers
instead of just bowing
my head in humble acceptance
for the divine grace,
even the divine lashings
of these difficult times,
at your divine lotus feet.

Grant me just one grain
of dust of your divine feet
to carry me across
the gap of maya delusion

to the heavens of God Realization
where I may know
you as God and Guru
and as myself.

I love you, my divine Guruji
May I have the loyalty,
faith and devotion,
will and discipline
to follow you
always.
Shining with love
you will carry me
across the gap.

I love you and
I lay my head
at your beloved
lotus feet
in total surrender.

RETURNING

Surrendering to this beautiful Stillness,
listening to Its sweet humming voice
Being inside Being
returning to the Centre
Always flowing
returning to You.

How could I forget You
You who are me.

Let the storms rage
for You move inside
each breath of wind.
Help me to dance my life
and be true to You.

SURRENDER

I asked how can I surrender?
The answer: there are always
risks in freedom
The only risk in bondage
is that of breaking free
But how do you break free?
How does the shoot come
out of the bulb?

It knows, for God gave it
its knowing
The oak-ness is in the acorn
so trust your true Being-ness
is in your self too
and just have faith
Continue living
and it will do its thing
through God's grace
The hands of the Master
will mould you
and play you to His divine tune.

Don't pull up the shoots
just allow the winter time
to bring on the Spring
Be patient,
Surrender!

YOU AND ME

You and me and me and You
locked in a dance
of everlasting joyous being.
Whispering I dissolve in
I love You!

WITH HOPE AND FAITH

With hope and faith
I lay my problems
at Your feet.
Comfort me and
wash away my tears.

Embrace me
and melt away
all my resistance
and guide me Home.

I love You
my Beloved One.
I am Your child divine.

YOUR FACE

Your face
so beloved
is so sweet
so encouraging
Your smile
forgiving
always.

Blue hues
of beloved light
herald Your
presence
softly
embracing
me
melting
in Thee.

RECEIVING

LISTEN

Listen – listen – listen
Listen for the silent whisper
of the Divine Voice within.
It is always there to guide you
and shine the light before you
so you won't stumble
on the rocks of ego.

Listen – listen – listen
to that sweet song within
whispering of the Beloved
waiting on the other shore.
Step in your boat of silence
and raise the flag of Love.
You are welcome there
where He waits.

He is listening, listening, listening
to your sweet heart song
Waiting, waiting, forever waiting
for you to return to Him
whispering you will never forsake Him
He will embrace you
in your soul song of silence.

YOU ARE CALLING ME

You are calling me
You want me to be near You
You want me to snuggle up
on your divine lap
and put my head onto Your breast
You want to hold my little hand
in Your loving guiding hand.

You love me with boundless love
You want me to know this
You want me to feel this
You yearn for me to come to You
as I yearningly have sought
for You in so many things
You waited patiently for me.

Now, You say, Now it is time
my beloved child
to come back to me.
The days of ignorance and separation
are running out
Your light is enveloping me
Your face is smiling inside me.

I love You.

YOU

It is You who are writing
Your poetry through Rumi, Kabir
and my Master's poems
It is You who spoke
in the beauty of the words of Christ and Krishna
It is You who paint the skies
and the trees and flowers on the canvas of life
It is You who smile at me
through countless faces
It is You who think in my mind
It is You who hold my pen
and write these words
It is You who sing the song of love
through devotional songs
to Yourself

O miracle of Life and Love
You, fathomless One
You and I are One
and in that Oneness
seemingly separated
I bow at Your holy feet
and see You reflected
in the smile of my Guru
in the love of Christ
In joyful gratitude
I lay my heart at Your feet

WHAT DANCE?

Thinking of the rhythm
of my life
what dance do I want
to dance?

Only a dance
in step with Your choreography,
the outlines You made for my life,
no other.

Help me to be in step
with You
and create a life of love
free of vices
and filled with virtues.

Let me shine
like a little light
in the firmament
of Your heavens.

Help me to listen
and hear Your guiding voice.
Not always rushing, busy
with life's tasks.

Help me to be still
in You
and find You within
in the ocean of my heart,
Thy heart.

WHISPERS OF LOVE

You shower me with Your love
daily, so many tokens
so many gifts
I whisper
thanks to You
with bowed head

My tears of suffering
flowing
over Your feet
I no longer cover my shame
Yet I love You, always love You
and in that love You return
Your love to me

You tell me
carry this cross
carry it for it will be over soon
In the intensity just before the end
My Christ felt forsaken
So when I feel alone
and cry out in despair
You and He and my Guru
You do understand

Then You respond and whisper so sweetly
"I love you" in my ears
and give me Your tokens of love
through the gifts
of life and my friends

THROUGH GOD'S LOVE

Through God's Love I was born
a child Divine,
Divine Love makes me breathe
Divine Love makes me grow
Divine Love makes me dance
The Dance of Life.

Forever growing onwards
Forever Being
Forever expressing
Divine Love.

I am new each moment
I am new today
Being and moving
a wave of the Infinite Sea
Being and moving
The Infinite Sea in a wave.

I open myself to my Inner Divinity
leaving all thoughts of smallness behind
Washing away the dreams of the ego
Awakening to the Light of my Soul
Through God's Love I am reborn
a Child Divine.

THOU EVERYWHERE

I walked in the rain
cold drops fell upon my face
and the wind blew.
Then a break came in the clouds
and the sunbeams fell
like light from heaven
down upon the earth.

The sun warmed my face
beautiful vistas opened
in the distance.
Hills and seas and skies
filled with beauty.

I walked and walked
then I turned
I gasped in joy.
Against the black sky
a perfect rainbow
a double archway as a gift.

The light a golden liquid
trees and fields
enveloped in Thy magic
Thou everywhere.

My heart sang with joy
I saw You
in trees, in light,
in grass, in colour,
in sky and rainbow
everywhere.

A greeting from You
in a little dog
that barked at me
with wagging tail.

I sang with my Guru
O, God beautiful
at Thy feet, O I do bow!
For You create such beauty
You are everywhere
How I love You
How I love You
my heart bursts
with love for You
in all everywhere
You Alone.

SWEET SECRET

Nothing has changed
yet all is different
all has a golden glow of joy
because You have touched me
and let me feel Your presence.

I put out my hand
and there You were
I found You in my heart
where You always have been
waiting for me
to discover this sweet secret.

I write this poem just for You
Just for You
because I love You
You, my Lord, just You!
I love You.

REMINDERS OF YOUR LOVE

I looked
into my friend's eyes
and I saw You.
It was Your love
that caressed me
and encouraged me
in her voice.
You my best Friend
in all my friends
in my husband
and the cat I stroke.
In the flowers
that smile at me
My orchids around the house
So many gentle comforts
and reminders of Your Love.

PEACE

All is well
All is peace
the spiral of life
embraces us in itself,
always connected
in the inner silence
of the eternal love
of God.

The movement finds its rest again
and I breathe out
letting go, setting free
I find strength again
and joy.

VREDE

Alles is goed
Alles is vrede
de spiraal van het leven
neemt ons mee,
altijd verbonden
in de innerlijke stilte
van de oneindige liefde
van God.

De beweging vindt weer rust
en ik adem uit,
loslatend, vrijmakend
vind ik weer kracht
en vreugde.

*In memory of my dear Mother
A Dutch translation of the poem Peace*

A WISH FOR YOU

May you always abide
in the beautiful Rose Garden
of your glorious Soul
where the Sound
of the Hidden Music
caresses you.

HIS ANSWER

I created you
a spark of Light.
No darkness
can touch your Beauty.
This Light
can never fade,
know that.

I created you
a Child Divine.
No darkness
can touch your Divinity.
Always
will I love you,
know that.

I created you
out of my own heart,
a wave of love.
No darkness can
pollute this Love.
You will always
be a part of my Oceanic Being,
know that.

I created you
with a silent smile,
a sound of joy.
No noise can
silence my voice
which whispers inside you
my guidance
to lead you back to me,
know that.

Know that
I always hold you
in the palm of my hand.
Never away,
always inseparably
within you,
as you are within me,
in my light.
Know That!

HIS SELFLESS LOVE

My Guru
Divine Messenger
Divine Helper
Sweet voice of God
sweeping me away
from the lashing sea
of Maya Delusion.
Carrying me across the gap
of earth and heaven
Showing me how to shine
with love
Radiating me
through His selfless Love
into God's Being.

I, YOUR CHILD

You stripped me of my
badges of honour
I cried out to You
You cannot strip me of one thing
that I am Your child.
I am Your child
I love You.

Then You came to me
and held me in such comfort
such peace and joy flooded
my being.
Being in You.
You and me
I, Your child
You, my father, my mother
You and me
You and me
You and me alone.

GRACE

Let me come and
sit at Your feet
and abide here
a while longer.

Let me bathe
in Your Light and
dwell with You
in Your beloved presence.

Baptize me
with Your blessings
and smile in my heart.

Shine Your joy
through my eyes
into the world.

Let Your touch
of love flow
through my hands.

Walk my feet
to those in need.

Whisper words of
comfort through my lips
to all I meet
through Your grace.

LOVING EMBRACE

After chaos
comes joy.
After the birth-pains
follows birth.

May I have the patience
of learning again
how to be
the new me
which is emerging
into a new blossoming.

A Spring waiting
to burst forth
after a long Winter.

May I have faith
to trust and to know
that You, my God
and Your angels
walk always
by my side,
whispering words
of encouragement
in my inner ears
and in my heart.

May I melt
in the sweet embrace
of my Soul
through which You
guide me along
day after day
with sweet love.

A love greater than the ocean
and softer than the sun's rays
which You lovingly shine on my face.
A love so tender
A love so fierce
A love all encompassing
A love eternal,
expressed in a loving embrace.

ENCHANTED

While walking in the woods
I saw a deer today.
She so gently stood there.
Then I saw him,
her beloved playmate,
hiding behind a tree,
peeping at me through the green leaves.

Enchanted, I thought of Thee.
You who are hiding from me,
yet watching me always.
Your loving nature created
these beautiful creatures.
You implanted them with Your
beauty and gentleness,
a gift of love to the other and
to us all, to me.

The deer transformed into You.
I saw You gracefully looking at me
as You lovingly played Your game,
Your Lila of hide and seek
with me.

THANK YOU!

I love You, Lord
Thank You for healing me
Thank You for Your light
Thank You for all the gifts
in my life
all the loving friends and people
all the comforts of life
my home and clothes and warmth and food
for my loving husband
for a comfortable bed to sleep in.

Thank You for my body
Thank You for You
for Christ and my beloved Guru
Thank You for this Sacred Path.

Thank You for the sun,
for the birds and flowers
Thank You for the trees
for light and darkness
for the moon and stars
Thank You, thank You, thank You
I love You, Lord.

Thank You for the gift
of my life
May I make my life
a gift of love to You and all.
May my prayers of love
create rainbows on Your firmament
of creation
May I be a pearl on Your string
of love in this world.

Thank You for creating me
May I shine as Your child
May I live in a corner
of Your divine heart
in eternal gratitude
to You, always
I love You,
my beloved Divine Father, Mother,
Eternal Friend.

MEDITATION

Your life is a Path towards complete
wholeness, harmony and unity.
Every aspect of your life and incarnation
is a step along this Path.
Each person, each event gives colour
and meaning to your journey.
The road has often not been easy to walk,
your feet were weary and torn at times,
yet you, warrior of God,
have come now to that part of your Path
where great Light is shining upon you!

Like the morning sun dispels the darkness of the night,
you can now see so much clearer where you are going
and the light at the end of the Path
is beckoning you, radiating
"Welcome, welcome Child of God!"
And you become aware
of the gentle hands on both your shoulders
and the sweet whisper in your ears
of the Shining Ones that guide you along,
overshadowed by the brilliance of your Soul.

How much love and welcoming there is
at this point on your journey
and with how much joy and faith

and trust and understanding
can you now go forward.

God, your innermost Friend,
has been there all along,
but like a blind one, you couldn't see His Light,
like a deaf one, not hear His soft voice
full of Love......
Now He has blessed you with vision and hearing
and you can meet His beloved Greatness
in which you exist inside,
for He is waiting there always.

Close your eyes and ears to the illusion
of the world and find Him
and your radiant self inside you
in the peace and stillness that awaits you there.
Feel yourself being filled with love
and hope and healing,
so you can now love yourself with the
Love of God inside
and love others with that same love
and see yourself reflected in all that is.
Just now enter deep into that beautiful,
still Centre within yourself
and rest there for a little while
and feel nourished and loved
and know that all is well!

TABLE OF CONTENTS

Longing 1

Like a Child 3
For You 5
My Longing for Thee 7
Like the Flute of Krishna 9
Ocean of Peace 11
Help Me to Shine 13
Teach Me.. 15
Embrace Me.. 17
Dance with Me 19
At His Feet 21
Speak to Me..23
How Many Times? 24
Be With Me 27
Climbing the Ladder 29
Let Me Be 31
Rescue Me! 32
Show Me Your Face 35
Thou and I 37
Sleepless Nights 39
To God! 41

Rebirth 43

On Wings of Light 45
The Miracle of Birth 46
United 49
New Beginnings 50
Naked 53
Like a River 55
A Thought Divine 57
Birthing 59
Burning the Dross 60
For Babaji 62
Free Yourself 65
Forgiveness 66
I No Longer Wish to Hide 69
Just You and Me 71
Great Mother 73

Loving 75

Gift of Love 77
In Gratitude 78
Living for Love 81
You Alone 82
Thy Word of Love 84
Song of Love 87
This Valentine's Day 89
Play Your Tune 91
May I Be Worthy 93

Indications of Love 95
Freedom from Fear..96
Embracing the Beloved 99
Blessing of Love 101
Ask and It Shall Be Given 102
A Smile Just for You 104
Anointment... 106
Only You! 109
Answered Prayer 110
My father, my Father 112
Rock Me Then 116
Silent Waves of Love 119
Thy Temple... 120

Surrendering 123

Be Still 125
On Wings of Grace 126
I Belong to Him.. 129
Great Dancer 131
Gifts of You... 132
Gently in My Soul 134
A Prayer.. 137
Do Dwell in Me.. 138
Die to This Self... 141
Attuning to the Highest.. 143
Crystals of Soul Lights.. 145
Dwell Where He Abides 147
My Guru, My Divine Friend....................................... 148

Returning 151
Surrender 153
You and Me 155
With Hope and Faith 157
Your Face 159

Receiving 161

Listen 163
You Are Calling Me 165
You 167
What Dance? 168
Whispers of Love 170
Through God's Love 173
Thou Everywhere 174
Sweet Secret 177
Reminders of Your Love 179
Peace 181
Vrede 183
A Wish for You 185
His Answer 186
His Selfless Love 189
I, Your Child 191
Grace 193
Loving Embrace 194
Enchanted 197
Thank You! 198
Meditation 200

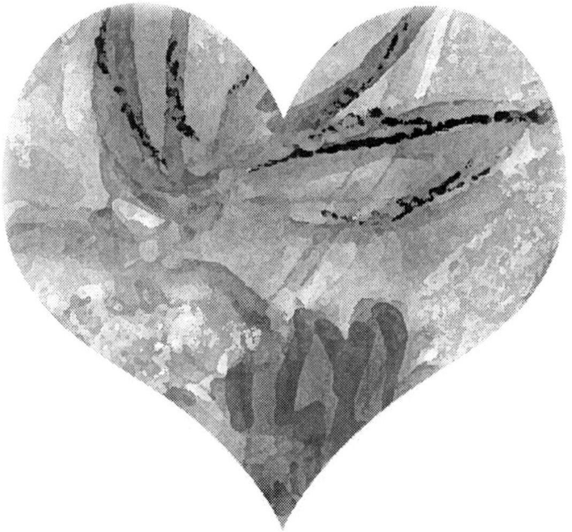

THERESIU JANICKI-HARDY

is of Polish-Dutch background and grew up in Holland, where she graduated in sociology and psychology with an MA in adult education. She worked as a lecturer in Holland before moving to England. Here she completed courses in spiritual psychotherapy and esoteric healing, psychotherapy, hypnotherapy and rebirthing. She holds a degree in fine art and danced for a number of years with the 5-rhythm groups of Gabrielle Roth.

Theresiu has been meditating for over 30 years and has a deep love for spirituality, which she has sought to reflect in her life and work, including her writing and painting. She loves nature and walking in the beautiful Sussex countryside where she lives.

She has been teaching meditation for the last twenty years. She has also been holding courses and workshops in self-awareness and esoteric and spiritual subjects and exhibiting her art work during this time. She has 25 years experience as a therapist and has run meditation groups and organized retreats for over 10 years, as a member of the Self-Realization Fellowship.

Theresiu continues to write and paint and hold meditation and spiritual development courses.

Lightning Source UK Ltd.
Milton Keynes UK
UKOW02f1257090115

244238UK00001B/116/P